The British Medical Association

FAMILY DOCTOR GUIDE *to*

BREAST
DISORDERS

▣ The British ✚ Medical Association

FAMILY DOCTOR GUIDE *to*

BREAST DISORDERS

MR. J. MICHAEL DIXON & MR. ROBERT C.F. LEONARD

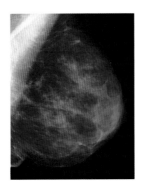

MEDICAL EDITOR
DR. TONY SMITH

DORLING KINDERSLEY
LONDON • NEW YORK • SYDNEY • MOSCOW
www.dk.com

IMPORTANT

This book is not designed as a substitute for personal medical advice but as a supplement to that advice for the patient who wishes to understand more about his/her condition.

Before taking any form of treatment **YOU SHOULD ALWAYS CONSULT YOUR MEDICAL PRACTITIONER.**

In particular (without limit) you should note that advances in medical science occur rapidly and some of the information contained in this book about drugs and treatment may very soon be out of date.

PLEASE NOTE

The authors regret that they cannot enter into any correspondence with readers.

A DORLING KINDERSLEY BOOK
www.dk.com

Senior Editor Mary Lindsay
Senior Designer Sarah Hall
Production Assistant Elizabeth Cherry

Managing Editor Stephanie Jackson
Managing Art Editor Nigel Duffield

Produced for Dorling Kindersley Limited by
Design Revolution, Queens Park Villa,
30 West Drive, Brighton, East Sussex BN2 2GE
Editorial Director Ian Whitelaw
Art Director Fiona Roberts
Editor Julie Whitaker
Designer Vanessa Good

Published in Great Britain in 1999 by
Dorling Kindersley Limited,
9 Henrietta Street, London WC2E 8PS

2 4 6 8 10 9 7 5 3 1

A CIP catalogue record for this book is available from the British Library

ISBN 07513 0684 3

Reproduced by Colourscan, Singapore
Printed in Hong Kong by Wing King Tong

Contents

Know your breasts

The breasts start to develop very soon after conception and, to begin with at least, do so in the same way whether the baby is a boy or a girl.

DEVELOPING AND CHANGING

Five or six weeks after a baby starts to grow, and while it is still only inches long, a ridge of tissue can be seen running from what will subsequently be the armpit to the groin. This ridge of tissue is called the 'milk line'.

Later, at about six months into the pregnancy, special secretory cells grow inwards from the baby's nipples, and channels (or ducts) are formed. By the time the baby is born, the breast anatomy is in place in basic form. In fact, some newborn babies have swollen or inflamed breasts as result of hormones passed to them through the placenta from their mothers.

Most girls' breasts start to develop between the ages of nine and eleven, but the process can begin earlier or later. Even when fully grown, the breasts are not capable of producing milk at this stage. It is not unusual for boys to experience some breast development during puberty as well, but this is only temporary and usually disappears within a year or two.

During pregnancy, a woman's breasts will get much bigger and may double their weight as milk-producing cells multiply and the system of ducts expands. The

THE CHANGING BREAST
The breast structure of a lactating woman changes in response to hormones released during pregnancy. The nipples enlarge and darken, the milk-duct system expands and more lobules are formed.

How the Breasts Develop

Breast development in females begins to occur around the age of 10–11 years, although it may be later. The ovaries produce oestrogen, leading to an accumulation of fat in the connective tissue, causing the breasts to enlarge.

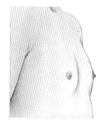 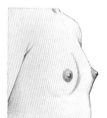 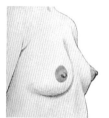 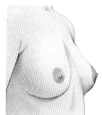

BEFORE PUBERTY THE
BREASTS ARE FLAT

AREOLAE DEVELOP
AS BUDS

BREAST TISSUE AND
GLANDS GROW

AREOLAE FLATTEN
OVER BREAST TISSUE

nipples get darker in colour and blood vessels become more prominent. All these changes take place in response to various hormones that a woman produces while she is pregnant and most are only temporary. However, once the nipples have become darker they will stay that way because they now contain more pigment than previously.

As we age, all our body tissues begin to lose their elasticity, and the breasts are no exception. They start to sag and, after the menopause, the fall in levels of the female hormone oestrogen causes the glands inside the breasts to shrink so they tend to get smaller.

INSIDE THE BREAST

The easiest way to understand how the inside of the breast is formed is by comparing it to an upturned bush. Its 'leaves' are known as lobules. They produce milk that drains through the 'branches' along a

The Anatomy of the Breasts

The breasts lie outside the ribcage and the pectoral muscles. They contain milk-secreting alveoli, and lacteal ducts carry the milk to the nipples. A network of lymph vessels and lymph nodes surrounding the breast forms part of the immune system.

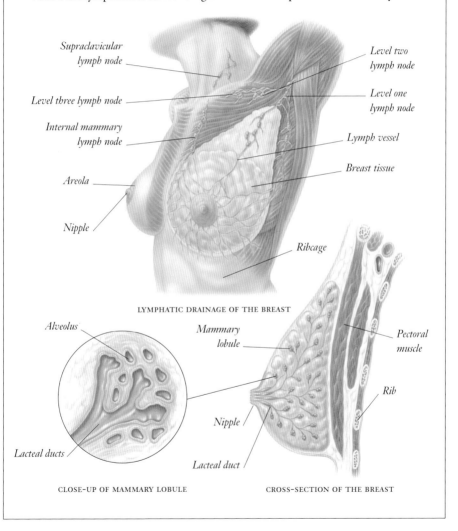

Supraclavicular lymph node

Level three lymph node

Internal mammary lymph node

Areola

Nipple

Level two lymph node

Level one lymph node

Lymph vessel

Breast tissue

Ribcage

LYMPHATIC DRAINAGE OF THE BREAST

Alveolus

Mammary lobule

Pectoral muscle

Rib

Nipple

Lacteal ducts

Lacteal duct

CLOSE-UP OF MAMMARY LOBULE

CROSS-SECTION OF THE BREAST

9

network of small ducts. These in turn drain into 12 or 15 major or large ducts that then empty onto the surface of the nipple. The nipple is the equivalent of the bush's trunk. As with a bush, the breast's branching network of ducts is irregular and not arranged symmetrically like the segments of an orange.

The part of the breast most susceptible to disease is the lobules. There are not many conditions that affect the ducts, and the few that do involve the major ducts underneath the nipple.

The spaces you would see in a bush between the leaves and the branches are filled inside the breast with connective tissue that plays a supporting role. Around all of this is a layer of fat between the milk-producing parts of the breast and the skin. The breasts are supported by the chest muscles beneath them, and toning up these muscles with the right kind of exercise is the only way to change your shape, apart from surgery. Exercise does not have any effect on the size or shape of the breast tissue itself.

BREAST AWARENESS

Women used to be advised to examine their breasts carefully and regularly each month at the same point in their menstrual cycle. Not surprisingly, doing this made some women feel anxious. Others felt guilty if they did not do it and they felt somehow responsible if they later developed a problem.

Today, most doctors agree that the really important thing is to know your own breasts so that you spot any unexpected change in them, and can seek advice straightaway. This is called 'breast awareness'. What it means in practice, is getting used to the appearance and texture of your breasts.

Taking Care of Your Breasts

The cycle of personal breast awareness and routine screening is the key to the early detection of any possible problems, more detailed examination of the breasts and early treatment for any disorder.

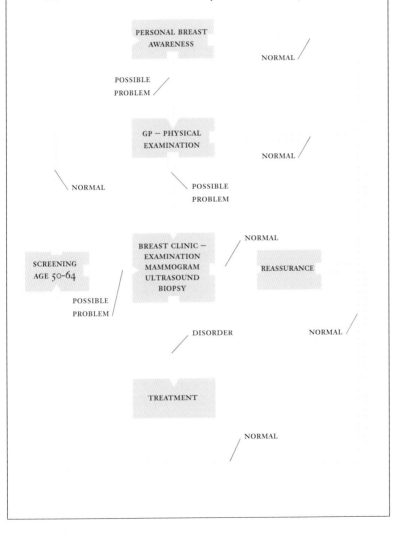

MIRROR INSPECTION
A basic awareness of how your breasts look in the mirror forms a good basis for detecting any general changes in their shape or skin texture.

First, you should know what your breasts look like. It sounds obvious, but it is a good idea to get into the habit of looking at your breasts in the mirror from time to time after a shower or bath or when you are getting dressed. Notice how they move up as you raise your arms and so on – so that you know what is normal for you. What you are looking for is a change in the shape of the breast such as a pulling in of the skin, any visible swelling of the breast or a change in the nipple, such as a pulling in.

You also need to know how your breasts feel. No one could be expected to find a lump when feeling her breast for the first time. You need experience before you can judge what is normal for you. Most women's breasts are a bit lumpy, especially in the days before a period is due. After your period this lumpiness becomes less obvious or may disappear altogether. Start by feeling your breasts every day for a few days until you are familiar with their texture and know how it changes through your menstrual cycle.

WHAT IF YOU FIND A PROBLEM?

You should see your doctor straightaway as soon as you notice any unusual change in your breasts – whether it is in the texture, the skin or the nipple. It is natural to feel anxious, but try to remember that roughly nine out of ten breast lumps are NOT cancerous.

Even if you do turn out to have a serious problem, there is absolutely no doubt that early diagnosis and treatment greatly increases the chances that the cancer will be cured completely.

KEY POINTS

- Be aware of the shape and feel of your breasts.
- Report any change in the shape of your breasts, or any lump that you feel, to your doctor.
- Even if you find a lump, nine out of 10 of these lumps are not cancerous.

Breast screening

*O*nce a woman reaches the age of 50, she will be invited to take part in the National Breast Screening Programme. This means having a mammogram, a special kind of breast X-ray, once every three years.

HAVING A MAMMOGRAM
During a mammogram, each breast is placed on a perspex plate and gently compressed. This flattens the breasts so that X-rays may be taken of as much breast tissue as possible.

You will be invited for breast screening until the age of 64 years and then, if you want to continue to be screened once every three years (and current evidence does suggest that screening over the age of 64 is worthwhile), you will need to make an appointment by phoning the breast screening unit or visiting the screening van when it is in your area. The aim of the screening programme is to pick up breast cancer while it is still small, and before it has had a chance to spread.

There are various reasons why women are not normally screened before the age of 50:

- Breast cancer is less common in younger women.
- Mammography is less likely to detect abnormalities because young women's breast tissue is denser than that of older women.
- There is no evidence that screening women before they reach 50 is cost-effective.

However, younger women who are thought to be at particularly high risk of developing the condition for some reason (see pp.58–61) are often offered screening at an earlier stage in their lives. This is usually mammography performed more regularly than that in older women, although there is a study that has started looking at whether a new type of scan (magnetic resonance imaging) is useful in screening young, high-risk women. In general, though, screening by regular mammograms is most effective in preventing death from breast cancer in women over the age of 50. Women are currently screened every three years in the UK programme as this appears to be the 'best buy' from a cost-effectiveness point of view. However, some research suggests that doing it every two years would pick up more treatable cancers, so anyone who is offered more frequent mammograms, e.g. at work, should accept.

MAMMOGRAPHIC SCREENING

You will be asked to undress to the waist and stand in front of the X-ray machine. The radiographer will then position each breast in turn between two perspex plates so that it is compressed and flattened. A brief pulse of X-rays is then used to take images of each breast – normally two per breast on the first visit and one or two on subsequent visits. Some women find the experience uncomfortable, and a few say that it is painful, but for the majority there is no more than minor discomfort. In any case, it is all over very quickly.

The X-ray film will then be examined and you will be told the results by your screening centre in around 10 days. A minority of women will be asked to return for a second mammogram, sometimes because

MAMMOGRAM
This colour-enhanced mammogram shows a normal breast in a woman of menopausal age.

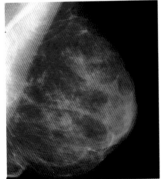

something has shown up that needs further investigation, or sometimes because of technical difficulties with the original X-ray. Remember that being recalled does not necessarily mean a diagnosis of cancer. Those who are recalled will see a doctor who will explain why the further check is needed.

LITTLE CAUSE FOR ANXIETY

Although most women are reasonably happy to go for a routine mammogram, being asked to go back for a repeat test or further investigations is likely to make you anxious.

This is natural enough, but it may help to keep the worry under control if you know that it is still unlikely that you will be found to have a serious problem.

The chart opposite shows what happens when 10,000 women are screened with breast X-rays. Of every 10,000 women screened, only around 55 are found to have cancer

INTERPRETING THE RESULTS
An experienced radiologist will scrutinise mammograms for any sign of abnormality.

and their chances of successful treatment are greatly improved because the cancer has been detected at a relatively early stage.

MAMMOGRAPHY – THE PROS AND CONS

- **Just having the test makes you anxious** Yes, but it does not last long and for the vast majority whose results are normal the relief makes it all worthwhile.
- **Supposing they miss something** It is very uncommon for a tumour not to be detected by mammography in women over 50.

Mammographic Tests for Cancer

Of every 10,000 women who are given a mammogram, 500 will be recalled for assessment; 100 of these will have a surgical biopsy and 55 will have cancers.

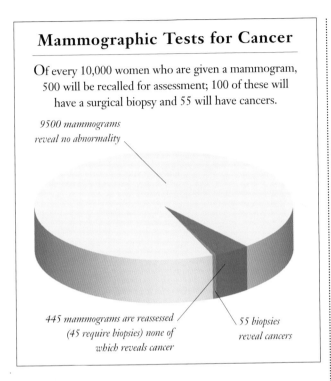

9500 mammograms reveal no abnormality

445 mammograms are reassessed (45 require biopsies) none of which reveals cancer

55 biopsies reveal cancers

● **A positive result is worrying and means more tests** In around five in 1000 screened an abnormality is found that, after further investigation, is found not to be cancer.

● **The X-rays might be harmful** Modern screening equipment delivers an extremely low dose of radiation and the chance a mammogram could cause a tumour to develop is very small.

● **Why suffer the worry and discomfort** On balance, the negative aspects of having a mammogram are very clearly outweighed by the real possibility that it could actually save your life. If you are one of the small minority of women whose mammogram does detect breast cancer, you will have a much better chance of successful treatment than if it were undiscovered and left to grow.

In those women who attend for screening, four of every ten women who would have died of breast cancer will survive the disease.

KEY POINTS

- All women between the ages of 50 and 64 are currently invited every three years for breast screening.
- Four of every 10 lives lost to breast cancer can be prevented in this age group by attending breast screening.
- After the age of 64, three-yearly screening is still recommended, but you will need to make your own appointment.
- Screening women under the age of 50 has not been shown to be cost-effective.

Seeing the doctor

Whenever you experience any symptoms relating to your breasts, the first person to consult is your GP. His or her priority is to decide whether there is a chance that you might have some serious disease within the breast and, if not, whether the problem can be sorted out without referring you to someone else.

If you have a definite lump or your doctor wishes to obtain further advice, you will be sent along to a hospital breast clinic. Alternatively, your GP may decide that your breasts should be checked again – perhaps at a different point in your menstrual cycle – and will ask you to come back for a follow-up examination.

VISITING YOUR GP
If you have any worries or symptoms relating to your breasts, you should consult your doctor straight away.

VISITING A BREAST CLINIC

The doctor will ask you to describe your symptoms in detail and also ask how long you have had them. If your problem is pain or a lump, he or she will also want to know if it varies in relation to your monthly cycle. You will then have a full examination. If you are seeing a male doctor, he will usually ask for a female nurse to be present during the examination.

19

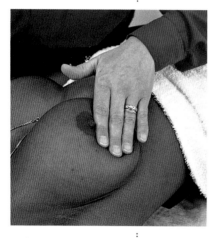

A PHYSICAL EXAMINATION
The doctor at the breast clinic will check your breasts for any lumps with his or her fingertips.

HAVING A PHYSICAL EXAMINATION

The doctor will look at your breasts, first with your arms by your side, then above your head and finally with your arms pressing on your hips. By looking carefully at the outline of the breast in these various positions the doctor can often see changes in the outline of the breast that will help to identify the site and cause of any complaint. Next, your breasts are examined while you are lying flat with your arms folded underneath your head.

If, during this examination, the doctor finds a lump, he or she will concentrate on this area examining it with the fingertips and measuring the lump. After checking your breasts, the doctor usually examines the lymph glands in the armpit and those in the lower part of the neck.

Should you need any further investigations, the breast specialist who sees you will tell you exactly what tests are needed and explain why they are necessary.

MAMMOGRAMS

If you are over 35 and have not had a breast X-ray within the past year, the clinic doctor will probably send you to have one done. This X-ray is known as a mammogram. For more on what happens when you have a mammogram, see pp.15–16. Some breast units actually arrange for patients to have their mammograms before being seen by the doctor in the clinic so that the X-rays are on hand when you attend the clinic. Otherwise, the film will be ready for the doctor to examine within a few minutes.

ULTRASOUND SCANNING

X-rays do not pass easily through the breasts of women under the age of 35. This often makes it difficult to obtain images of sufficiently good quality because the breasts are too dense. Ultrasound, which is familiar to many women because it is used to look at babies during pregnancy, can also be used in the breast to tell whether a lump in the breast is filled with fluid (cystic) or whether the lump is solid.

Ultrasound is not useful as a screening test, and is really only of value in patients where there is an abnormality on the X-ray or where there is a definite lump. When a lump is solid, ultrasound is an accurate means of judging whether it is benign and straightforward or whether it may be more serious.

NEEDLE TESTS

Inserting a needle into a lump will show whether it is full of fluid (a cyst) or solid.

The needle used for these tests is small – the same size as the ones used to take blood. As the breast is very sensitive, the needle test can be uncomfortable, but it does not take long to do.

If the lump is found to be solid, a few cells can still be sucked out for examination under the microscope to find out whether the lump is benign or whether it is a breast cancer. If the doctor is fairly sure that the lump is solid, then an alternative is to remove a small portion of the lump with a slightly larger needle, called a core biopsy needle.

Before this test is carried out, the skin and the surrounding tissue are numbed with local anaesthetic. Provided that the local anaesthetic has been injected

21

What Happens in Fine Needle Aspiration

Fine needle aspiration is a procedure used to withdraw sample cells from a breast lump. A small syringe needle is inserted directly into the lump. If fluid is withdrawn, then the lump is a cyst. If the lump is solid, a sample of cells is removed for microscopic examination.

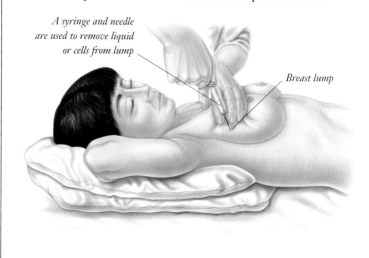

A syringe and needle are used to remove liquid or cells from lump

Breast lump

in the right place, it is not a painful test. When the anaesthetic wears off, however, the area where the breast has been sampled can be tender and patients are usually advised to take painkillers, the same as those that are used for a headache, such as paracetamol or ibuprofen (Nurofen).

If the doctor who sees you is happy that there is no serious abnormality in your breast, then he or she will reassure you and tell you that you do not need to come back any more.

If you have had a needle test or an X-ray, you may be given another appointment to come back for the results. In some clinics you may able to wait and get your results the same day.

As well as a doctor, you may also see a specialist breast care nurse while you are at the clinic. She will check to make sure that you understand what the doctor has told you and may help in arranging follow-up appointments and further tests.

Do not hesitate to tell the nurse if you are worried about anything in particular or if you have any questions that have not been answered by the doctor. The nurse should have enough time to talk over your concerns, and either be able to answer any questions you may have or to get the doctor to answer these questions for you.

SEEING A BREAST NURSE
A specially trained breast care nurse will explain any necessary tests and treatments to you, as well as answer any questions and worries that you may have.

FOLLOW-UP VISITS

You will be given a follow-up appointment if you need to come back to get the results of tests. If they indicate that there is no problem in the breast, then you will not usually need to see the doctor again. If, however, the tests suggest that the lump might be serious, the doctor will explain what this means.

Sometimes the results of the tests are such that it is not clear exactly what is wrong, in which case you may need to have further investigations.

If you have had a simple needle test, but this has not shown the cause of the lump, then it is possible that at your second visit you will have a core biopsy, which is described on pp.21–22.

Points of Biopsy Incisions

When a biopsy is carried out, the incision is usually made along natural tension lines in the skin to help keep any scarring on the breast down to a minimum.

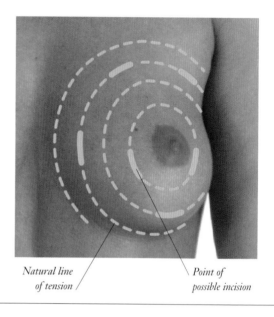

Natural line of tension

Point of possible incision

Alternatively, a doctor may suggest that the lump be removed. This is called an excision biopsy, and it can be performed either while you are awake, under local anaesthetic or more commonly under a general anaesthetic. Before any operation, you are asked to sign a consent form agreeing to the removal of the lump. It is important for you to know that the doctor performing the operation will only remove that lump and will not take any more tissue away without explaining the procedure to you first and getting your consent.

WHAT DO THE TESTS MEAN?

Needle tests are very accurate and are rarely ever wrong if they show cancer. Occasionally, the mammogram or ultrasound scan will be reported as showing a cancer but, when it is tested with a needle or removed and analysed, it turns out to be non-cancerous.

This might happen in one out of 20 cases. This is why the doctor will often tell a woman that a lump might be cancer, but that it is impossible to be 100 per cent certain until it has been tested with a needle or removed and analysed.

The combination of performing a careful examination, doing X-rays and/or scans and removing cells with a needle for testing is very accurate and, if you have all these three tests, it is very rare to miss a cancer. If all the tests show that a lump is not serious, then it does not necessarily need to be removed.

KEY POINTS

- Your doctor will examine you if you report a breast problem. If the doctor wishes to obtain further advice, you will be referred to a breast clinic.
- At the breast clinic, you will be examined and may have the following done: a mammogram, a breast ultrasound scan or a needle test.
- The combination of examination, X-rays or scans and a needle test is very accurate in identifying the cause of a breast lump.
- Not all breast lumps need to be removed.

Nature's mistakes

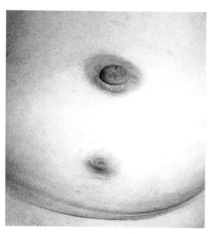

As we saw in the section on developing and changing breasts on pp.7–8, the ridge of tissue called the milk line normally disappears before birth. Occasionally, a part of the ridge that should have disappeared remains and forms an extra nipple or, occasionally, an extra breast.

EXTRA NIPPLE
Some people are born with an extra nipple, which commonly looks like a mole. These can be removed if they cause distress.

Extra nipples are common – between one and four in every 100 people have one. They are usually situated below the normal breast on the milk line, while extra breasts are most common in the armpit. These extra nipples or breasts can be affected by the same diseases that affect ordinary breasts. An extra breast that is causing problems – whether physical or psychological – can be surgically removed if necessary.

BREAST SIZE

In theory, breast size does not matter at all; it has no bearing on a woman's sexuality or on her ability to breast-feed. In reality, however, concern about breast size is a source of very real distress to many women. It does not necessarily help them to know that breasts naturally come in many different shapes and sizes, or that their own breasts are well within this normal range. It is not at all unusual to have one breast noticeably larger than the other, with a bigger left breast being more common. The difference may not be obvious to anyone else, but if the discrepancy is very marked, it can be corrected by surgery. Either the smaller breast can be made larger, or vice versa.

Very large breasts can cause women a lot of problems. Apart from the embarrassment factor, which can make life particularly difficult for young women, large breasts may be painful. Their weight puts a strain on a bra's shoulder straps so they cut into the skin. Many women suffer a lot from backache as a result of large breasts. They can get in the way of ordinary physical activity and can be a real handicap when it comes to games and sport. Any woman troubled by difficulties like this should talk it over with her doctor. It may be worth considering surgery to reduce the size of her breasts. The operation, called reduction mammoplasty, can be done on the NHS and can make a very real difference to a woman's quality of life. It is not considered purely cosmetic surgery these days because the effect on a woman's physical and psychological well-being is often dramatic and very worthwhile.

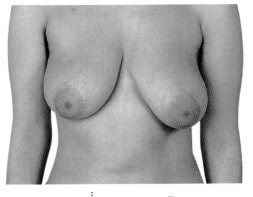

ASYMMETRICAL BREASTS
It is very common for one breast to be larger than the other. The difference is usually not very noticeable, but if it is, and this causes embarrassment, corrective surgery may be performed.

Small breasts do not cause the same kind of problems as large ones, although individual women may be very concerned that their breasts are too small. However, it is extremely rare for surgery to increase breast size to be available on the NHS, so anyone who wants her breasts enlarged is likely to have to pay.

Breast Reduction Surgery

An operation to reduce the size of the breasts is done under a general anaesthetic and will probably take up to four hours of surgery. It is a fairly major operation and generally involves some degree of discomfort for several days afterwards.

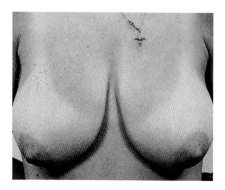

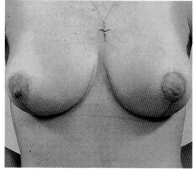

BEFORE SURGERY   AFTER SURGERY

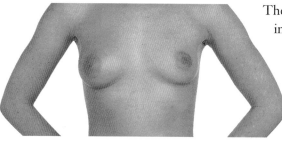

TINY BREASTS
Small breasts may be upsetting to the individual concerned, but enlargement surgery is rarely available on the NHS.

The operation to enlarge the breasts involves inserting implants behind the breast tissue. The most commonly used implants are made of silicone. There was a question mark over the safety of these silicone implants in the USA, but a team of British specialists concluded that silicone implants do not do any harm, and that there is no reason for any women who have them to be concerned.

There are alternatives to silicone that include salt water and soya bean oil. Neither of these produce as good a result as silicone. Even though the operation to enlarge breasts is not being done on the NHS, it is still worth asking your GP for advice if you are considering it as he or she may be able to recommend a good surgeon or clinic. It is still possible to breast-feed after you have had breast implants.

The most common complication after insertion of implants is the formation of capsules around implants. The capsules contract down and result in hardening, and this can cause pain, discomfort, change of shape and embarrassment. Rupture of the implants is a major concern among patients. About 10 per cent of the earlier varieties with thinner envelopes are liable to rupture after 10 years. In fact, ruptured implants cause very few problems, because almost all the silicone remains within the fibrous capsule formed by the body. Newer implants are less likely to rupture.

RETRACTED NIPPLES

Some women have naturally retracted or "pulled-in" nipples, which is not at all significant in health terms. However, some women feel this is an embarrassing 'abnormality' and it can cause problems when it comes to breast-feeding. There is a device available from chemists, called Nipplette, which has been reported to be successful in resolving this in some women. It is possible to correct the problem with cosmetic surgery, although you will have to have this done privately. When you are pregnant, wearing breast shells may encourage your nipples to protrude normally (see p.48). It is possible to correct the problem and in many parts of the country this can be carried out on the National Health Service.

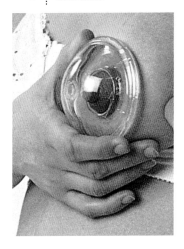

BREAST SHELL
Using a breast shell encourages retracted nipples to protrude, making breast-feeding much easier.

NIPPLE PIERCING

This is now reasonably common. The problem is that the ring can cause damage to the ducts underneath the nipple, and this can result in recurrent infections or leakage of material from the duct through the skin. If this happens, the ring should be removed and the area allowed to settle.

MALE BREASTS

All men have some breast tissue under the skin and, like that of women, it does respond to hormonal changes in the body, although much less dramatically. Other factors, including some drugs and occasionally other illnesses, may cause breast swelling, but usually the situation resolves itself without the need for anything beyond a medical check-up.

Sometimes, a boy or a grown man may notice that he is starting to develop a breast shape that is more like that of a woman. It is actually not uncommon in boys between 10 and 16 years old – affecting between one- and two-thirds of boys during puberty. It might seem alarming but is actually nothing to worry about at all and will almost certainly disappear quite naturally in time. However, if it is noticeable enough to be really embarrassing or if the swelling has not begun to subside after two years, it is worth seeing your GP.

The same thing can sometimes happen in middle and later life, and a man between the ages of 50 and 80 who notices any breast swelling should tell his GP.

BREASTS IN ELDERLY MEN
Hormonal changes in older men may cause their breasts to grow. Most breast swellings in elderly men are harmless, but a doctor should be consulted.

Normally, no treatment is needed, but a mammogram may be necessary first to rule out any possibility of a malignant growth. One per cent of cancers in men are breast cancers.

KEY POINTS

- Extra nipples and extra breasts are common.
- Large breasts can cause considerable problems, and surgery to make them smaller is available on the NHS.
- Small breasts can be made larger using breast implants.
- Enlargement of male breasts, which can be embarrassing, is common in boys between the ages of 10 and 16, but usually disappears within a year or two.

Breast pain

About five million women in the UK get breast pain, known medically as mastalgia. A survey carried out among women who work at Marks & Spencer found that 40 per cent had experienced breast pain recently and, of those with pain, just over one in five women said it had been severe.

LIVING WITH BREAST PAIN
For some women, breast pain can be so severe as to disrupt daily life, though it is rarely a sign of serious disease.

More often than not, breast pain is not that bad, and many women simply accept it as a normal feature of the changes brought on by their menstrual cycle.

As a general rule, we think of pain as a sign that there is something wrong, perhaps even a serious problem, but this is rarely the case with breast pain. Breast cancer is, in fact, usually painless. At one time it was thought that women who were worriers or who were depressed were more likely to complain of breast pain, but studies have now shown that there is no such connection.

TYPES OF BREAST PAIN

Breast pain can be divided into two types:

• **Cyclical** This kind of pain is worse immediately before a menstrual period

• **Non-cyclical** In this case there is no association between the pain and the time of the month.

If you are not sure whether your breast pain follows a regular pattern, it is worth keeping a diary for a couple of months. You could ask your GP to let you have one of the standard charts for recording breast pain, or simply make your own. On it, you need to note each day how bad the pain is (say on a scale from 1–5), and mark the days when you have your period. You could also record other details, such as any dietary changes, stressful events and so on. After a while, the diary should help you decide whether your breast pain is cyclical and whether there are other contributory factors for you.

CYCLICAL BREAST PAIN

Symptoms that come and go according to the time of the month are a familiar feature of many women's lives. You may become more aware of your breasts, perhaps because they feel full, heavy and uncomfortable or become lumpy and tender, usually around 3–7 days before your period starts. Women who have become used to this often go to their GP because they begin to experience actual pain in the breasts before a period for the first time. This problem is more common in women in their 30s, but it can also happen in older women if they are taking hormone replacement therapy. Otherwise, it usually disappears after the menopause, but being pregnant or taking the Pill does not generally make any difference, and it can continue for many years.

You may find the pain is not the same every month, but most women describe it as a heaviness or an ache, rather like toothache, with the breast feeling tender when

KEEPING A DIARY
Writing down any incidences of breast pain, making a note of the dates, will help you to determine if your breast pain is cyclical or not.

touched. It usually affects the outer half of the breast. Certain movements can increase the pain – this is particularly important if your daily life involves using your arms or lifting a lot. Unless they've experienced it for themselves, many people do not realise how bad breast pain can be or how seriously it can affect your life.

WHAT CAUSES CYCLICAL BREAST PAIN?

Despite the fact that cyclical breast pain occurs each month before a period, research has failed to show up any differences in hormone levels between women who experience bad breast pain and those who do not. Women with breast pain have been found to have some abnormality in the level of certain fatty acids in the blood. It may be that lifestyle factors – such as smoking, caffeine intake and diet – play a role, but what this might be is not yet clear.

CAN IT BE TREATED?

Your GP will probably want to give you a thorough examination to make sure there is nothing obviously wrong. Most women with mild cyclical breast pain do not need any treatment as such, although it is worth seeing a trained bra fitter to make sure you are wearing the

WEARING A SPORTS BRA
This type of bra will often help alleviate breast pain as it provide good support to the breasts.

right size and type of bra – a firm, supportive bra of the kind recommended for sports wear can often relieve the pain.

Your doctor can also reassure you that cyclical breast pain has no connection with breast cancer – something that is at the back of many women's minds and naturally worries them. Mild breast tenderness that starts just before your period is due and disappears after it finishes is rarely, if ever, a symptom of any underlying disease.

WILL EVENING PRIMROSE OIL HELP?

For a minority of women – about 15 per cent – the pain is so severe that it disrupts their lives and interferes with everyday activities. If you are one of these, there are various treatments that your doctor will consider. He or she is most likely to suggest evening primrose oil to begin with. You will probably be prescribed 6–8 capsules of Efamast 40 or 3–4 capsules of Efamast 80 to be taken every day for three months initially. This is long enough to assess whether you are one of the two-thirds of women whose breast pain does respond to treatment with evening primrose oil. If it is working, you should carry on with the capsules for another three months, then stop taking them. There is a 50 per cent chance that, when you stop taking the evening primrose oil, the pain will then have disappeared and will not return. If it does come back, again there is a 50 per cent chance that it will be much less severe than before. However, for the unlucky 25 per cent of women who find their breast pain is no better, another six-month course of Efamast may do the trick. Side-effects with evening primrose oil are very few and minor (see the chart on p.39).

WHAT DRUG TREATMENTS ARE AVAILABLE?

If evening primrose oil does not work and the pain is severe, there are other possible approaches to treatment. A variety of drugs is available that work by

Checking the Fit of Your Bra

Wearing a bra is good for your breasts. When you choose a bra, make sure that it fits correctly and supports your breasts.

- Make sure your bra fits around your body flat and is not too tight. Too tight a fit will be uncomfortable and could cause breathing difficulty. The bra should lie close between your breasts and not stand away from your body.
- See that the bust is fully contained within each cup; sometimes gaping at the side means that the cup is too small. If the cup wrinkles all over it shows that the cup is too large.
- If the breasts bulge along the top of the cups, the cups are too small.
- Bulges at the armpits mean the bra size is too small.
- Check that flesh is not bulging over the top of the cups, under your arms and across the back. Make sure that there is no flesh bulging beneath the band.
- If the bra is underwired, the underwiring should lie flat against your body, following the contours of your body and not dig into your breast. A soft cup bra will fit differently to an underwired bra, because the wire contains your breast whereas it can spread in a soft cup bra.
- If your bust is heavy, the bra's straps should be wide and strong enough to support it. Make sure that the rest of the bra is helping to support the bust.
- The cup 'spacing' should be correct. Make sure your breasts lie naturally, not pushed to one side or the other.
- Always test the fit of your bra both standing and sitting. The breast tends to 'plump up' when seated; this is especially noticeable in a strapless bra.

Choosing a Bra

When you are choosing a bra, make sure that is has adjustable straps and fittings, and that it gives you the correct amount of support. Ask for expert advice from a fitting specialist, if necessary.

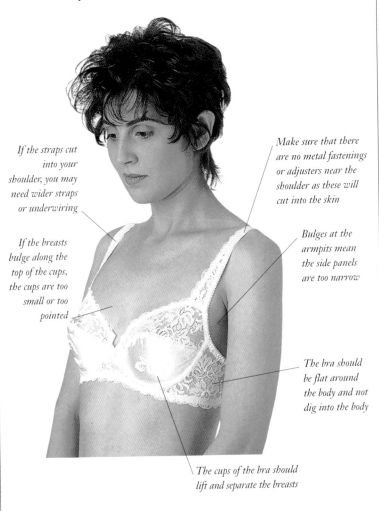

If the straps cut into your shoulder, you may need wider straps or underwiring

If the breasts bulge along the top of the cups, the cups are too small or too pointed

Make sure that there are no metal fastenings or adjusters near the shoulder as these will cut into the skin

Bulges at the armpits mean the side panels are too narrow

The bra should be flat around the body and not dig into the body

The cups of the bra should lift and separate the breasts

interfering with the hormones that act on the breast. They include danazol, bromocriptine and tamoxifen. Although they are sometimes more effective than evening primrose oil, they all have more side-effects so it is important to weigh up the pros and cons with your doctor before starting to take any of them. However, it is worth remembering that any side-effects will disappear once you stop the course of treatment. The side effects are summarised in the chart on p.39.

● **Danazol** This is very effective in treating breast pain, and often works when evening primrose oil has failed and when the pain is very bad. Danazol works against the sex hormones, by blocking the release of two hormones from the pituitary; it reduces the amount of hormones produced by the ovaries and so reduces the amount of circulating oestrogen, which is thought to be one of the major hormones to cause breast pain. However, as with bromocriptine, you cannot take this drug at the same time as the oral contraceptive pill, and you must use a mechanical alternative, such as condoms, a coil or a cap.

● **Bromocriptine** This drug is now rarely used in the treatment of breast pain because of its side-effects. It works by reducing the amount of one of the hormones that acts on the breast – prolactin that plays a role in production of milk. There is now a newer drug that reduces the amount of prolactin in the body, called cabergoline. This is taken once a week and as yet does not have a licence to be used in breast pain, but trials are in progress.

● **Tamoxifen** May be used occasionally to treat severe breast pain but only in exceptional circumstances. Tamoxifen interferes with the female hormone oestrogen,

Possible Side-effects of Treatments

All the side-effects of breast pain treatment are reversible – that is, they disappear when the treatment is stopped – but you will not necessarily get any or all of them.

TREATMENT	POSSIBLE SIDE-EFFECTS
Evening primrose oil	Occasionally: stomach upsets, greasy skin and hair
Danazol	Oily skin, acne Occasionally: deepening of the voice
Bromocriptine	Nausea, giddiness
Tamoxifen	Hot flushes

by stopping oestrogen reaching its target cells. It therefore has the same effect as danazol and reduces breast pain.

WHAT OTHER TREATMENTS MIGHT HELP? Although sometimes tried in the past, various treatments now known not to work include antibiotics, water tablets (diuretics) and vitamin B6. Although no particular oral contraceptive pill has been linked with breast pain, some women find it helps to change to a brand with a lower progestogen content. Others find the pain improves if they stop the Pill altogether and use an alternative means of contraception. Starting HRT can sometimes bring on breast pain and lumpiness that usually settles down after a while, but can remain a problem for some women. In these

women, evening primrose oil is usually effective in controlling the pain and lumpiness.

HOW CAN YOU HELP YOURSELF?

Keep a diary to record when your pain comes and goes and note down any factors that seem to play a part. Try the various strategies listed below one at a time and see if each one helps. If you try them all at once, you will not know which are responsible for any improvement.

● Get your bra size checked by a trained fitter; buy a couple of supportive, sports-style bras and, when your breasts are painful, wear one day and night.

● Start taking some regular aerobic exercise.

● If you're a smoker, make up your mind to stop.

● Experiment with your diet: some women find that avoiding fried and fatty foods and drinks containing caffeine and cutting down on salt can all be helpful in relieving breast pain.

NON-CYCLICAL BREAST PAIN

Women who experience this type of breast pain tend, on the whole, to be older than those whose pain is cyclical, with an average age of 43. The pain of non-cyclical mastalgia can arise from the breast itself, from the muscles and ribs under the breast or from sites outside the breast.

You may feel it as one or more tender spots over your ribs, next to the breast bone or over the ribs just outside your breast. This type of pain is actually coming from the muscles or the ribs. It may be there all the time but, more often, it comes and goes without any regular pattern.

EXERCISE
Some women find that regular aerobic exercise helps alleviate their breast pain.

Women usually describe the pain as burning or drawing, but it can sometimes be stabbing in nature.

CAN TREATMENT HELP?

Before the doctor can offer you any treatment, he or she needs to identify where precisely your pain is coming from. If the source can be pinpointed to a specific area on the chest wall as is often the case, you may be given either an anti-inflammatory cream or gel to rub in or an injection of a local anaesthetic and a steroid.

Non-cyclical pain coming from the breast itself is often eased by a simple painkiller, such as ibuprofen. It can also help to wear a well-fitting supportive bra day and night. If these simple measures do not help, your doctor may think it worthwhile trying you on evening primrose oil (Efamast capsules, see p.35). Although they do not work as well as for women with cyclical breast pain – only about half as many respond to treatment – they have very few side-effects.

The drug treatments used for cyclical breast pain, such as danazol, can also be tried in extreme cases, but they do not work as often for non-cyclical pain and of course they have more side-effects than evening primrose oil (see p.39).

KEY POINTS

- Breast pain is very common.
- It is not a frequent symptom in women with breast cancer.
- Wearing a firm supporting bra can help relieve the pain.
- Pain that comes and goes in relation to the menstrual cycle usually responds to treatment with evening primrose oil.
- Hormone replacement therapy can cause breast pain in older women.
- Pain that is not related to the menstrual cycle is best treated by simple painkillers.

Breast infection

This most often affects women between the ages of 18 and 50, but is much less common than it used to be. Although they can occur at any time, many breast infections happen while a woman is breast-feeding her baby.

BREAST-FEEDING

Infection is most likely to be a problem during the first six weeks of breast feeding, although some women develop it while they are weaning their babies. Although it can be treated effectively, it is far better to prevent it altogether if possible. If you have any problems getting your baby to breast-feed happily and comfortably, seek the advice of your midwife, breast-feeding counsellor or health visitor.

BREAST-FEEDING INFECTIONS
Nipple infections in lactating mothers are common during the early weeks of breast-feeding. The breast becomes hot, reddened and painful.

The first symptoms of a breast infection are pain, swelling, redness and tenderness and you may start to feel quite unwell, with a raised temperature, general aches and pains and a headache, almost as though you had flu. You may well have been aware, before the infection set in, of a cracked nipple or a break in the nearby skin. If you have also had a problem with one of your breasts becoming engorged because the milk was not being drained properly, this makes an infection more likely. This happens because the milk flow that normally washes away any harmful organisms does not occur when there is reduced flow of milk. Many mothers find their babies feed more easily from one breast rather than the other – often the left breast if she is right-handed and vice versa. This can mean the other, less popular, breast is not completely emptied and so is more prone to engorgement and infection.

If you suspect you have developed an infection, you should see your doctor as soon as you can. You will probably be given a prescription for one of the antibiotics that can be taken safely while breast-feeding. It is important that you carry on feeding your baby from the infected breast, as draining the milk from it completely will reduce the chances of an abscess forming. Your baby will not come to any harm from the bacteria in your milk, as they will be easily killed off by the acid in his or her stomach. If you cannot carry on feeding for any reason, you should express the milk from the infected breast, either by hand or using a breast pump.

If the infection does not settle quickly on antibiotics, then it is likely that an abscess has formed and your GP will send you to

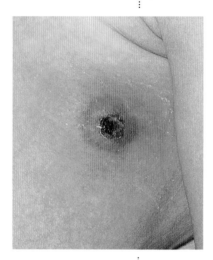

BREAST ABSCESS
An abscess is a collection of pus in the breast tissue and is caused by an infection. An abscess may cause tenderness, and, if close to the skin, inflammation.

hospital to have it drained. This can often be done in the out-patient clinic using a local anaesthetic, but some doctors prefer the woman to have a general anaesthetic, although this is not ideal when you have a young baby to look after. These days, the draining may well be done using a fine needle to withdraw the contents of the abscess (localised collection of pus). This procedure, called aspiration, may need to be carried out more than once. Until recently, an abscess would have been cut open surgically and this alternative method is still sometimes used. Once the abscess has been drained, you can carry on with breast-feeding, and there is no reason why you should have similar problems in future.

OTHER BREAST INFECTIONS

Women who are not breast-feeding sometimes develop an infection, usually in an area close to the nipple. Most of them are in their late twenties or early thirties and around 90 per cent are smokers! It seems that something in cigarette smoke somehow damages the major ducts beneath the nipple and the damaged area then becomes infected. The condition, known as periductal mastitis, causes pain and redness in the area around the nipple and sometimes there will be an underlying lump.

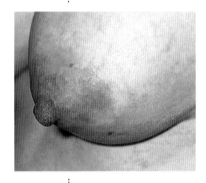

PERIDUCTAL MASTITIS
Non-lactational mastitis causes pain and redness around the nipple. It is more common in women who smoke than in non-smokers.

Normally, antibiotics get rid of the infection, but if not, then an abscess has probably developed. When this happens, you will have to go to hospital to have the abscess drained (see p.44).

Unfortunately, because draining the abscess does not remove the damaged duct, you are quite likely to find that the problem recurs. Sometimes, the duct is so severely damaged that a hole develops that allows fluid from the duct to leak through the skin and stops it from healing. This condition is known as a mammary duct fistula. If you develop this problem or suffer repeated bouts of infection, you may need a small operation to remove the damaged ducts and solve the problem for good.

It is not unknown for a woman to develop an infection in another part of the breast, away from the nipple, although it is not as common. However, when it does happen, this type of infection usually responds well to treatment with antibiotics.

SKIN INFECTIONS

Some women who have large breasts may find the skin on the underneath of their breasts becoming infected. This happens because the skin of the breasts is in permanent contact with the skin of the chest wall or abdomen, which produces heat and sweating. This makes the skin an ideal breeding ground for bacteria, which then set up an infection.

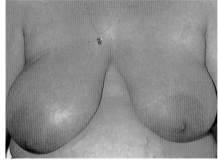

LARGE BREASTS
Women with very large breasts sometimes suffer from a skin infection on the undersides of their breasts where this skin is in constant contact with the skin of the abdomen.

Usually the problem can be treated with an antibiotic either orally or as a cream that you rub into the affected area. You will be advised to keep it as clean and dry as possible. This means washing twice a day and dabbing the skin gently dry with a cotton towel or using a hair dryer instead. You should avoid using talc or body lotion and either opt for cotton bras or wear a cotton T-shirt or vest inside the bra next to the skin. If the cream and hygiene measures do not work, it may mean you have a deeper infection that will need treatment with antibiotics in tablet form. If you are overweight, you can reduce the chances of the infection recurring by losing weight. However, if you are normal weight but simply have very large breasts, it may be worth considering whether you could benefit from surgery to make them smaller (see pp.27–28).

KEY POINTS

- Breast infection during breast-feeding is now uncommon but can be a problem during the first six weeks.
- If you suspect that you have an infection, visit your GP as soon as possible for antibiotics. You can continue to breast-feed even if you are taking antibiotics.
- Infection around the nipple in non-pregnant women is usually associated with smoking.

Nipple problems

Problems with nipples are relatively common, but fortunately most of them are not at all serious.

NIPPLE SHAPE

Some people have nipples that are naturally retracted, which is not at all important unless you want to breast-feed, when it can cause difficulties. It often helps to wear breast shells inside your bra while you are pregnant as this will encourage your nipples to protrude and make feeding your baby easier.

If your nipples change shape and become indrawn or pulled to one side as you get older, you should let your doctor know.

Often, this will prove to be just a normal feature of ageing, as the major ducts under the nipples get shorter and wider. As they become shorter, they pull the middle part of the nipple in, often producing a slit effect across the nipple. Sometimes, as the ducts shorten and widen, they fill up with a cheesy material that may leak out through the nipples (see p.50). Your doctor will probably want you to have a check-up at a breast clinic, where you will be examined and have a breast X-ray to make sure everything is normal and there is no lump behind the nipple. Occasionally, a pulled-in nipple may be a sign of inflammation in the ducts underneath the nipple.

PREPARING FOR FEEDING
Pregnant women who have inverted nipples and wish to breast-feed, may benefit from wearing nipple shells inside their bra.

48

For women whose nipples change shape or become indrawn, a mammogram is usually necessary to exclude the possibility of cancer. Once any serious underlying disease has been ruled out, however, you can be reassured that the change in your nipple shape is nothing to worry about.

NIPPLE DISCHARGE

A discharge usually comes through the nipple from the ducts underneath, but it may sometimes come from the surface of the nipple itself. The word discharge sounds like something unpleasant but, in fact, two-thirds of women who are not pregnant can be made to produce fluid from the nipple simply by cleaning it and massaging the breast. A common form of discharge is a milky discharge that can continue to leak from the breasts long after a woman has finished feeding her baby – perhaps for months or even for years. Much more rarely, a woman may start to produce milk from her nipple even though she is not, and has never been, pregnant.

All women, even if they have never been pregnant, have fluid inside their breasts, but it does not normally find its way to the outside because the ducts are blocked with plugs of a substance called keratin. Vigorous exercise or sexual activity may dislodge these plugs and so release fluid in a discharge that comes and goes. The fluid, which may come from one or both breasts, usually only appears in small amounts and may range in colour from white to pale yellow to green to blue/black. In all cases, it is perfectly normal and nothing to worry about.

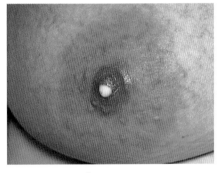

MILKY DISCHARGE
The breasts can sometimes secrete milk in a woman who is not breast-feeding.

49

Discharge that is a symptom of duct disease tends to be more troublesome, appears in larger quantities and is there all the time. A yellowish or blood-stained discharge is most likely to be caused by a wart, known as a papilloma, in one of the ducts underneath the nipple. Discharges that are blood-stained, persistent or troublesome are easily treated by removing the abnormal duct. This is a very simple operation performed through a very small incision around the nipple, and it is very successful at getting rid of the discharge.

A thicker, cheesy discharge can also occur in older women whose ducts widen with age and become filled with cheesy material that can leak out onto the surface of the nipple.

It is also possible to suffer from a discharge from the skin surrounding the nipple rather than from the nipple itself. Some women have trouble with eczema on the aureola, the skin around the nipple. Although the cause is not clear, the treatment is simple – using a very dilute steroid cream.

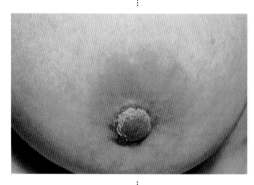

PAGET'S DISEASE
This rare form of breast cancer involves the milk ducts of the nipple.

Another possible cause of discharge from the nipple is a disease of the skin of the nipple known as Paget's disease. This causes an ulcer on the surface of the nipple and is usually a sign that there is a cancer or pre-cancer present in the breast. As a result of this, women with discharge from the surface of the nipple or from the surrounding skin need to have a careful breast examination, plus mammograms and, if necessary, samples of skin and tissue from your breast may be taken for microscopic examination. If tests show Paget's disease, then an operation is usually required. The operation can either be removal of the nipple and tissue underneath the nipple, sometimes followed by radiotherapy, or it can be treated by a mastectomy.

KEY POINTS

- Problems with the nipples are common.
- Pulling in of the nipple can be the result of infection, ageing or cancer.
- Most discharge from the nipple is not serious.

Lumps and cysts

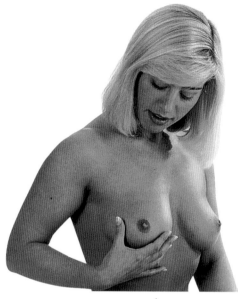

Most breast lumps are not cancerous. In fact, all women have lumpy breasts, and many of the lumps that women find are just lumpy areas of normal breast tissue that become more prominent and are often easier to feel just before a period is due.

BREAST LUMPS
If you notice a lump in your breast, it is likely to be one of the two common benign types – a fibroadenoma or a cyst. These lumps, which are harmless, are part of the normal changing growth pattern of breasts.

Lumpy breasts used to be known as fibrocystic disease, and having lumpy breasts does not make you more likely to develop breast cancer. Only if you notice a new, distinct and separate lump do you need to report it to your doctor.

FIBROADENOMAS

These lumps are not strictly speaking a disease at all; rather they are overgrowths of the 'leaves' described on pp.8–9 – the breast lobules. They account for six out of 10 lumps found in women under the age of 20, and it is relatively unusual to develop another one later in life. Ultrasound and fine needle aspiration (see pp.21–23) are usually used to confirm the diagnosis, but once your doctor is sure that the lump is a fibroadenoma you may not need any actual treatment. At least one in three will get smaller or disappear

52

on their own within two years, but if you're worried, or if the lump is getting bigger, you can opt to have it removed.

CYSTS

Cysts are swollen lobules that can form as breast tissue ages, which is why they mostly affect women in their 30s, 40s and 50s. They are especially common in the years before the menopause. We do not know what causes cysts, but it is not just a blockage of the draining duct.

Most cysts are smooth, mobile lumps; some are large enough to be easily visible and they can be painful. It is usually quite easy to identify a cyst with ultrasound and mammography. The final and definitive investigation is conveniently also the treatment for a cyst. The doctor inserts a fine needle into the lump, with no anaesthetic, and extracts the fluid from inside the cyst and usually the lump disappears completely. The fluid may be yellow, green or blue/black. If the fluid is blood-stained it will be sent for tests because, very occasionally, a cancer may form in the wall of a cyst, but this is rare. Cysts that produce blood-stained fluid are usually removed.

Of every six women who develop a cyst, three will never have another one. Two of the six will have between three and five cysts during their lifetime and the remaining woman will have more than five. The good news is that it is not necessary to have a cyst drained every time, provided the doctor is confident that it is a cyst rather than a solid lump. Women who have had one or more cysts are not at significantly increased risk of developing breast cancer – there is some risk, but that risk is not considered to be significant.

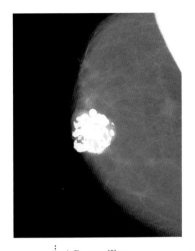

A BENIGN TUMOUR
This mammogram shows a fibroadenoma, a non-cancerous tumour. Fibroadenomas commonly arise in the breasts of young women under the age of 20 years.

KEY POINTS

- Most lumps are not cancerous.
- The most common cause of a lump in a young woman is a fibroadenoma.
- Fibroadenomas do not need to be removed.
- Cysts are more common in women in their 30s, 40s and 50s, and they are treated by inserting a fine needle and removing the fluid.
- Benign lumps are not associated with a significantly increased risk of breast cancer.

Breast cancer

More women get breast cancer than any other type of cancer – around one in 12 will have the disease at some point in their lives. A woman's risk of developing breast cancer doubles every 10 years, and it is actually very rare in younger women.

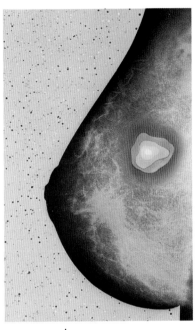

Despite its relative rarity in younger women, breast cancer is the most common cause of death in women between the ages of 35 and 50, although it is true that many women, including those under the age of 50, are successfully diagnosed and treated. It is also worth remembering that nine out of 10 breast lumps are found to be benign, or non-cancerous. Of those that do turn out to be malignant, or cancerous, the earlier they are detected and treated, the better the woman's chances of survival.

EARLY DETECTION
This false-colour mammogram reveals the presence of a breast tumour, seen here as a yellow area. The earlier cancer is detected, the better the chance of long-term survival.

WHY IS CANCER A PROBLEM?

A lot of cells in the human body are growing at any one time, but their growth is very carefully controlled so that the number of cells that are produced matches the number of cells that are dying. A cancer consists of cells that are growing and dividing at a faster rate than cells are dying, so that the group of cells that form the lump gets bigger and bigger. As the lump increases in size, so some of the cells develop the ability to move away from the lump and get to other parts of the body through the bloodstream. This is called spread (metastasis) of a cancer, and some of the cells that get into the bloodstream start to form new lumps in different areas of the body. If the cancer cells grow in important areas, such as the lungs, the liver or the brain, or if the cells involve a lot of different bones, then this can cause major problems.

WHAT ARE THE RISK FACTORS?

It is not a simple matter to try and work out your personal level of risk because so many factors play a part in determining who gets breast cancer. In any case, an individual has little or no control over most of the risk factors. What you can do if you face a higher than average risk is to take advantage of screening programmes and visit your doctor promptly if you suspect you may have a problem.

Even if you know you are more susceptible to breast cancer than the next woman, any lump you find is still more likely to be benign than malignant.

Experts have worked out some of the factors that seem to make it more likely that a woman may develop breast cancer, but it is worth bearing in mind that, even if all of them were relevant to one particular woman, she still might not get the condition.

- **Getting older** More women in the older age groups develop breast cancer, with a doubling of risk every 10 years.
- **When your periods begin and end** Starting early and going on beyond the age of 55 seem to be linked with increased risk.

- **Postponing pregnancy** Women who do not become pregnant until after the age of 30, or who never have children, are at greater risk than those who are pregnant for the first time in their teens.
- **Breast-feeding** A woman who has breast-fed one or more children has a lower risk than a woman who has never done so.
- **Abnormal breast cells** A few women who have had a non-cancerous condition are found to have an abnormality in certain breast cells that makes later cancer more likely. Although this is not common, a woman with this problem, known as atypical hyperplasia, will need regular check-ups. Other types of non-cancerous breast problems do not increase your risk of developing cancer.
- **Overweight** Being seriously overweight, greater than 1.5 times the average weight for your height, does increase breast cancer risk. There is also a link between breast cancer and eating a diet that is high in fat, but no one is yet sure quite how this operates.
- **Drinking and smoking** Some studies have shown a link between drinking alcohol and breast cancer, with women who drink a lot having a higher risk than those who either drink no alcohol or drink it in moderation. Smoking has not been directly linked to breast cancer risk, but its implication in other diseases and effects on your general well-being cannot be over-emphasised.
- **Taking the Pill** There is a very slightly increased risk for women while they are taking oral forms of contraception. The risk is short-lived and disappears 10 years after stopping the Pill.

OBESITY AND RISK
Overweight women have an increased risk of developing breast cancer.

● **Taking hormone replacement therapy** For the first 10 years, the health benefits outweigh the slightly increased risk of breast cancer, but after that the risk becomes more important. For a woman of 50, over the next 20 years she has a one in 22 chance of developing breast cancer that increases to one in 20 if she takes hormone replacement therapy (HRT) for 10 years. The risk goes up to one in 17–18 for 15 years of use.

The decision on whether to keep taking HRT beyond 10 years is an individual one, based on the pros and cons for each individual woman. Hormone replacement therapy is usually only given to a woman with a strong family history of breast cancer if she is having major problems with the menopause.

● **Family history** One in 10 women who develop breast cancer have inherited some kind of genetic abnormality that makes them more susceptible to the condition. There are various ways of identifying women with this kind of risk – see the information box opposite.

If you are seeing your doctor about a breast problem and know that several of your family have had cancer, not just breast cancer, it is important to find out as much as you can about what happened. It would be useful to know what type of cancer they had, at what ages they developed it and, if relevant, at what ages they died.

Relationship of HRT to Breast Cancer Development

The incidence of breast cancer among women over 50 who are taking HRT increases with the length of treatment.

TIME ON HRT	EXTRA CANCERS IN HRT USERS
Never	–
5 years	2 per 1,000
10 years	6 per 1,000
15 years	12 per 1,000

Breast Cancer Families

Some women have a greater than average chance of developing breast cancer due to some abnormality in their genetic make-up. The risk may be increased if any of the following apply:

- Several members of her family have or have had breast cancer.
- She has relatives who developed breast cancer while under the age of 50: the earlier in life it happened, the greater the risk that it was caused by an inherited abnormality.
- She has relatives who have had cancer in both breasts or who have had certain other types of cancer, particularly cancer of the ovaries, colon and prostate, while young, which can be caused by the same gene that causes breast cancer.

Cancer genes can be inherited from either parent, even though neither of them may have actually developed cancer themselves. No one yet knows how many breast cancer genes there are, but five have been identified so far. About one in three cases of inherited breast cancer is thought to be due to an abnormality in a gene known as BRCA-1, and the same proportion to another gene called BRCA-2, with the other three genes and a number of undiscovered genes being responsible for the rest. Testing for abnormal genes is currently available only in certain centres. Before any woman can be offered a test, it is necessary for the doctor to show that somebody in the family who had breast cancer had an abnormal gene.

Women who come from such affected families may then be given the opportunity to find out if they are carrying the abnormal gene and are at increased risk. Women who carry an abnormal gene have between a 60 per cent and 85 per cent chance of actually developing breast cancer at some time in their lives.

Family History and Incidence of Breast Cancer

Breast cancer can affect successive generations of women in a single family, suggesting the presence of a strong hereditary factor. Given her family history, the woman at the bottom of this family tree has decided to undergo genetic tests.

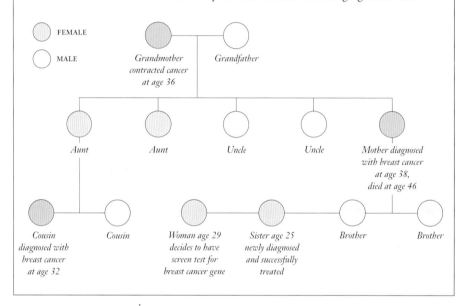

Before opting for the genetic test, women should be aware that the finding of an abnormal gene could make it difficult to obtain life assurance (and maybe a mortgage). This is why women having the test are offered counselling before and after it.

If, having had the test, a woman is found to be carrying an abnormal gene, then she may wish to take steps to reduce the risk of breast cancer actually developing. Usually this will mean starting regular intensive screening at an earlier age, or alternatively in women whose family history suggests that they are very high risk, or whose gene test shows that they are carrying an abnormal gene, can opt for a double mastectomy and breast rebuilding (reconstruction), or can enter one of the ongoing drug prevention studies to try to prevent breast cancer developing.

As you can see there is not much anyone can do to avoid many of the risk factors. However, it is worth trying to get your weight down if you need to, and cutting down on fat in your diet, as this will also reduce your risk of developing heart disease.

HOW IS A DIAGNOSIS MADE?

The first indication that something is wrong may be the woman herself noticing a lump or change in a breast or it may be picked up by her GP or at a routine mammogram. It is very important for you to be aware of how your breasts normally feel and look so that you will spot any change quickly. Of course, you must follow up any such observation by going to your GP.

Any woman who finds a lump or other abnormality in her breast is bound to be worried, but the sooner you get it properly checked out, the better.

The chapter Seeing the doctor, on p.19, explains in detail what happens when you go to your GP and what tests may be required when you have a breast problem that needs investigation (see pp.20-25). As a reminder of the way things usually work, the flow chart (see p.11) summarises the various stages you might go through.

KEY POINTS

- Breast cancer affects one in 12 women in the UK.
- A woman's chance of getting breast cancer doubles with every 10 years of her life.
- Up to 10 per cent of women who develop breast cancer have inherited an abnormal gene that puts them at increased risk of developing this condition.
- Women at high risk are usually offered screening, starting at a younger age.
- Genetic testing is not widely available and is not easy to perform.
- For the first 10 years of taking HRT, the benefits outweigh the slightly increased risk of developing breast cancer.

Extent and kinds of breast cancer

Many people do not realise that breast cancer is not just one disease that is always treated in the same way and that has the same predictable outlook for everyone who gets it.

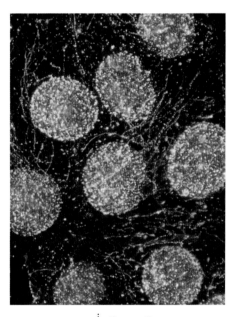

There are several aspects of breast cancer that play a part in determining how well the person will do and whether her outlook is likely to be better or worse. Factors that must be taken into consideration include the size of the tumour, whether it is the type that has the potential to spread outside the breast, what the tumour looks like under the microscope and so on.

CANCER CELLS
This light micrograph shows cultured human breast cancer cells, magnified 64 times.

 ## ASSESSING THE PROBLEM

Breast cancers develop from the cells that line the breast lobules and the draining ducts. Cancer cells that are confined to the lobule and the ducts are called 'in situ' or 'non-invasive'. They are also sometimes referred to as 'pre-cancers', in recognition of the fact that they do not have the ability to spread to other parts of the body that most people associate with cancer. An invasive breast cancer is one where the cells have moved beyond the ducts and lobules into the surrounding breast tissue.

Non-invasive cancer can turn into invasive cancer if left in the breast untreated. Invasive cancers do have the ability to spread and they are able to enter lymph channels in the breast and spread to the lymph glands under the arm – this is the most common place that they spread to or from which they can get into the bloodstream and spread elsewhere in the body. The lymph system is involved in fighting infection and is a network of lymph channels and lymph glands throughout the body. If a germ gets into the body, it passes through the lymph channel to the lymph glands where the cells that are involved in the killing of germs are stored. Cells in the lymph glands either themselves kill the germs or produce substances called 'antibodies' that are released into the bloodstream. The lymph glands that drain the breast are under the arms, so when the cancer cells get into the lymph channels they move to these glands.

Both non-invasive and invasive cancers are also further subdivided according to other criteria. In the case of invasive cancers, the most important distinctions are in the different ways they grow and spread and the type of cells involved.

When a cancer is examined under the microscope, it may be possible to assess how aggressive it is likely to be – in other words how far and how fast it is likely to spread. Following this type of analysis, a tumour may be assigned to one of three grades – ranging from grade I to grade III in order of seriousness.

Rather than being one disease, breast cancer is in fact a whole lot of separate diseases. It may be easier to understand if you think of breast cancer in terms of dogs: at one end of the spectrum is a small cancer of a so-called 'special type' of cell that behaves much like a small, well-trained family pet. At the other extreme is a large cancer of cells of no special type that behaves more like an uncontrollable rottweiler. The aim is always to find out what type of tumour an individual has and tailor the treatment to suit the cancer.

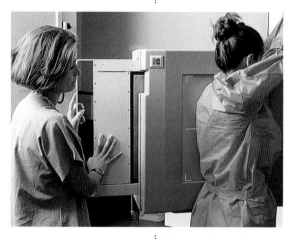

One more thing doctors need to know before treatment can be started is whether the cancer has spread and, if so, how far. If breast cancer is diagnosed, you will normally have a thorough clinical examination, blood tests and a chest X-ray to check that there is no evidence of cancer elsewhere in the body and to check your general fitness for surgery.

HAVING A CHEST X-RAY
Before starting any treatment for breast cancer, you will have a general examination, including a chest X-ray.

Occasionally, the doctor may decide to do a bone scan to check all your bones and a liver scan to look in detail at your liver. This information allows the doctor to assess the stage of the cancer and the best way in which to treat it.

This process is known as 'staging' the cancer, and distinguishes three main groups.

● **Early** This describes cancer that seems to be confined to the breast and/or the lymph nodes of the armpit on the same side of the body.

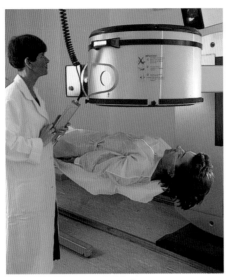

CANCER SPREAD
Scanning with a gamma camera is a technique used to look for evidence of spread of the cancer to other parts of the body.

• **Locally advanced** Cancer that has not apparently spread beyond the breast and armpit but is best not treated initially by surgery. In locally advanced breast cancer, the skin of the breast is usually abnormal and is either swollen or red, or the cancer is growing directly into the skin. These cancers used to be treated by surgery first, but it was found to be successful only in about 50 per cent of all patients; in the others the cancer came back in the areas next to where the surgery was performed.

• **Advanced** Cancer that has spread beyond the breast and armpit to other parts of the body.

KEY POINTS

- There are many different types of breast cancer.
- Cancer cells confined to lobules and breast ducts are called in situ or pre-cancer.
- The most common site for an invasive cancer to spread is the lymph nodes under the armpit.

Treating breast cancer

Once a thorough assessment has been made, it is then possible to work out the most appropriate treatment. This might include surgery, radiotherapy, hormone therapy, chemotherapy or a combination, depending on the cancer itself and taking into account the individual woman's wishes.

TREATMENT OPTIONS
It is very important to discuss all treatment options with your doctor once breast cancer has been diagnosed.

When the possible treatment options have been explained to you, you will be invited to share in the decisions about what is to be done, although of course some women prefer to leave such decisions to their doctors.

In most cases, treatment is likely to involve surgery alone or surgery and radiotherapy to deal with the cancer in the breast and the glands under the arm, followed by drug treatment aimed at destroying any undetected cancer cells that may have escaped into other parts of the body.

Of all cancers, breast cancer is one of the most treatable, and it is associated with a high cure rate. Treatments for breast cancer are improving and so is survival. Despite the fact that more women develop breast cancer every year, the number who actually die from breast cancer is falling, demonstrating the effectiveness of current treatments.

SURGICAL REMOVAL

When the lump is relatively small (under four centimetres in size), it is usually possible for the surgeon to remove it along with a small amount of the surrounding tissue (breast-conserving surgery). With a larger lump, this breast-conserving operation may not be worthwhile because so much of the breast would have to be taken away to get rid of the cancer. In some women with relatively small breasts, who have lumps under four centimetres in size, then sometimes when the lump and some surrounding tissue are taken away it may not be possible to leave enough breast tissue to make saving the breast worthwhile.

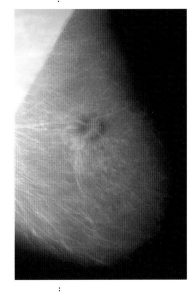

In fact, about one in three breast cancers cannot be removed in this way, and are best treated with mastectomy – an operation to remove the whole breast, usually including the nipple. Fortunately, surgical technique has improved dramatically since the days when a so-called radical mastectomy – removing all the tissue right down to the chest wall – left the woman with a serious deformity of the chest and arm and damaged her ability to use her arm normally. You may possibly know or be told about someone to whom this has happened, but there is no cause to worry that the same thing might happen to you if you need to have a mastectomy. These days, some women actually choose to have a mastectomy

SAVING THE BREAST
This mammogram shows a small cancerous breast tumour. Small lumps such as this can often be surgically removed, leaving the breast intact.

69

Different Types of Breast Surgery

The extent of surgery necessary in breast cancer depends on the size, location, outline and nature of the cancerous tumour. A surgeon will attempt to remove the minimum amount of tissue necessary to get rid of the cancer.

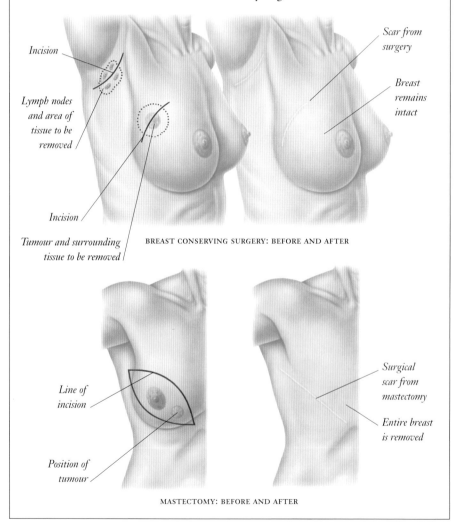

Incision

Scar from surgery

Lymph nodes and area of tissue to be removed

Breast remains intact

Incision

Tumour and surrounding tissue to be removed

BREAST CONSERVING SURGERY: BEFORE AND AFTER

Line of incision

Surgical scar from mastectomy

Entire breast is removed

Position of tumour

MASTECTOMY: BEFORE AND AFTER

even though they could have a simple lump removal. There are also certain situations where a woman with a lump smaller than four centimetres may be advised to have a mastectomy. The main ones are:

• When there is more than one lump in the breast. Research shows that, even if all these lumps are removed, other cancerous lumps are quite likely to develop later in other parts of the same breast.

• When the cancer is directly under the nipple so that it would have to be removed at the same time. Rather than leave the breast without a nipple, it is sometimes better to take the breast away altogether and have a breast reconstruction – see pp.72-75.

• Sometimes, an operation to remove the lump is not entirely successful, because either some cancer or pre-cancer is left behind. Another operation to remove more tissue may solve the problem but it might be necessary to remove the whole breast.

• Sometimes, the tissue surrounding the lump may be abnormal and on its way to becoming cancerous. If it cannot all be removed by a wide excision, a mastectomy may be the safest option.

The surgeon normally removes some or all of the lymph glands from under your arm. There are about 20 of them and they are the most common place to which the cancer may spread. Knowing whether this has happened and, if so, how many of these glands are affected is important both in assessing the severity of the cancer and in deciding on the drug treatment. If the surgeon just needs to see whether the cancer has moved into these glands, removing either a single gland which drains the cancer or a few of them is usually sufficient but the only way to find out how many have been affected is to remove all of them. Where tests on one or only a few of the glands that have been removed during surgery show that they have been affected by cancer, the remaining lymph glands need to be treated with radiotherapy. In any case, most women will have a course of radiotherapy after breast-conservation surgery even if the glands are not affected (see the section on radiotherapy on pp.75-77).

Sometimes, surgery in the armpit can cause damage to the nerves in the upper arm so it feels numb afterwards. This is obviously a nuisance but it does not usually last long. Around one in 20 women who have all their lymph glands removed or who have had them treated with radiotherapy develop lymphoedema or swelling in the arm. Treatment can usually reduce the problem, although it cannot always be got rid of completely. Massage can help, as can wearing an elastic stocking, and it is worth propping your arm up on several pillows while you are sitting down. It is also important to avoid injuries or infection in your hand – from gardening, for example – as this can leave you with worse swelling even after the infection has cleared.

BREAST RECONSTRUCTION

If you have decided with your doctor that your cancer is to be treated with a mastectomy operation, the surgeon will probably discuss with you the possibility of having breast reconstruction surgery done at the same time. The operation is often more successful if done straight away rather than if it is left until months later. There is no evidence that immediate reconstruction makes a recurrence of cancer any more likely nor that, if it should come back, it will be harder to detect.

Breast Reconstruction Using Implant

After breast surgery, a patient may opt for reconstructive surgery. One type of surgery involves inserting an implant under the skin. This is expanded over several months by injecting saline solution into it.

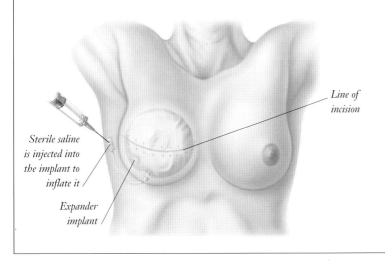

Line of incision

Sterile saline is injected into the implant to inflate it

Expander implant

HOW IS RECONSTRUCTION DONE?

The simplest method is to insert an implant under the skin, but this usually needs to be combined with some means of stretching the remaining skin to make up for the amount that was removed during the mastectomy operation. This may be done in two stages, so that the skin is expanded before the implant is inserted or a combined expander and implant can be used. The idea is that the expander is gradually inflated with injections of fluid over a period of months to stretch the skin, in much the same way as the growing fetus stretches the skin of a woman's abdomen during pregnancy. When this process is complete and the skin has expanded enough, the device can either be removed and replaced with a permanent prosthesis or implant, or some fluid can be removed leaving the smaller, breast-sized implant in position.

Most implants consist of a plastic (Silastic) shell or envelope filled with silicone gel. Older implants had a very thin shell and small amounts of silicone would occasionally leak out of these. Newer implants have a much thicker outer shell and are much less likely to leak any silicone. The body produces tissue around an implant, called a capsule and, even if the implant does leak silicone, in all but a few women the body contains all the silicone within this capsule. Very occasionally, the silicone can leak into the surrounding tissues and cause irritation and scarring.

Many medical devices placed into the body contain silicone and these include artificial joints and heart valves. Any silicone that gets into the bloodstream can occasionally find its way to other parts of the body, but even at this stage it does not seem to cause significant problems. There is, for instance, no evidence now that silicone, when it leaks, causes joint problems or any other disease. Alternative implants are available that contain salt water or soya oil. Around one in 10 women experiences problems with implants because the capsule around the implant tightens or hardens and causes the implant to change shape, and this may be painful.

The original implants had a smooth surface, but the newer implants have a rough, irregular (textured) surface and these textured prostheses are associated with a much lower incidence of hardening.

Occasionally infection may develop, although the chances are considerably reduced by giving the woman antibiotics during and after the operation.

An alternative to using artificial implants alone is to bring skin and muscle from another part of the body to replace the lost breast. This may be taken from the back or from the abdomen. When the 'back flap' method, using a muscle called the latissimus dorsi, is chosen, an implant is usually needed in addition to the muscle to create the appropriate size of breast. Sometimes it is possible to transfer fat as well when the muscle from the abdomen is used, so an implant is not then usually necessary.

The main disadvantage of using this approach is that the transplanted tissue does not always survive. About one in every 100 back flaps and one in every 20 abdominal flap operations fail in the end for this reason.

Whether the surgeon uses muscle or an implant to reconstruct the breast, it is possible to reconstruct a nipple at a later time. This is done either by transplanting some darker coloured skin from the upper inner thigh or by tattooing the skin to create an areola. Alternatively, a simpler solution is to opt for one of the very natural-looking stick-on nipples now available.

RADIOTHERAPY

There is good evidence to show that all women who have had breast conservation surgery do benefit from radiotherapy treatment afterwards but it is only needed in about a quarter of patients after a mastectomy.

Radiotherapy kills cells that are growing. In a normal breast, only a few cells are actually growing at any one time, but a cancer consists of cells that are growing all the time. Radiotherapy, therefore, has its greatest effects on cancer, although it inevitably produces some slight damage to other tissues that can result in slight scarring of the breast.

HOW IS RADIOTHERAPY DONE?

You will probably be asked to come to the outpatient clinic each weekday for four or five weeks to have the radiotherapy. It only takes a few minutes each time and is completely painless. It is a bit like having an X-ray and you do not need to worry that it will make you radioactive – it won't! Before you are given the first dose, the area to be treated is marked on your skin using a semi-permanent dye. This is so that whoever is giving the treatment can be sure you are in exactly the same position each time, and you will be asked to keep absolutely still while it is being done.

After a few days of radiotherapy, your skin may look red and feel a bit sore, rather like you have spent too long in the sun. Towards the end of treatment you can also get some blistering of the skin. As when you put water onto sunburned skin, it can make the skin sore, some radiotherapists prefer patients to keep the treated areas dry and just to apply creams. Other doctors are quite happy for you to get this area wet. You should follow the advice given by your own radiotherapist as he or she will have decided what is best for you. You should also protect the treated area from the sun. Nowadays, there are very few side-effects from radiotherapy, for instance it does not make your hair fall out and it does not make you sick, although towards the end of the treatment you can feel slightly tired. Some patients who get radiotherapy to the breast do get a slight cough and this is caused by the fact that when you give radiotherapy to the breast you also give some to part of the lung immediately under the breast. This can cause slight scarring of the lung, which causes irritation and results in a cough or, very occasionally, you might be slightly breathless. There are specific treatments for this, so if you experience these problems just report them to your own doctor.

FOLLOW-UP APPOINTMENTS

If you have had breast conservation surgery, you will probably have to go for a check-up every six months for a year or two and then for a yearly check, and you'll have a mammogram of both breasts every one to two years. If you have had a mastectomy, your check-ups will probably be every six months for the first year and then annually, with mammograms of the other breast every 1–2 years.

DRUG TREATMENTS

An advantage that drugs have over other kinds of treatment such as surgery and radiotherapy is that drugs reach all parts of the body. This means that they can act on cancer cells that have spread, but in such small numbers that they cannot be detected. As a result, they can prevent cancer recurring for months or even years after treatment. If cancer is already widespread by the time it is first diagnosed, drugs may be the only practical way of treating it.

The drug treatment used for breast cancer falls into two main categories: hormones and chemotherapy.

HORMONES

Most breast cancer is affected by hormones, and mainly by oestrogen. The other natural hormones that affect breast cancer are progestogens. At low levels they do not seem to have much influence, but, when given to patients at high doses, progestogens can make breast cancer shrink as effectively as any other hormonal manipulation, such as removing oestrogen or by using anti-oestrogens (see p.79).

It is possible to determine whether a tumour is sensitive to hormones by doing a chemical test on tumour specimens, taken at biopsy. Most breast cancers are actually oestrogen sensitive. There is a tendency, however, for younger patients to have a slightly higher incidence of hormone-insensitive cancers and a tendency in older patients (women after the menopause) to have a high incidence of hormone-sensitive cancers.

● **Oestrogen-sensitive tumours** In women who have passed the menopause, about two out of three have oestrogen-sensitive tumours, but the proportion goes down to one in three of younger premenopausal women. These hormone-sensitive cancer cells have receptors on their surface that react to oestrogen, causing the cells to multiply more quickly.

Tamoxifen is a drug that works by blocking the effects of oestrogen on the tumour. In some patients this results in tumour destruction, in others in prevention of further growth of the tumour. Either of these effects can be of great benefit in controlling the disease and removing the symptoms of the cancer. The effect of tamoxifen may last for many months or years in individual patients, although it is impossible to predict just how long the effect can last.

The only really serious side-effect is that tamoxifen can double the incidence of endometrial cancer in the lining of the womb. There is no doubt that this risk has been over-emphasised in the media and the actual risk is very low. As long as tamoxifen is stopped within five years, the risks of endometrial cancer developing are extremely low.

Most of the evidence suggests that the optimum length of time to take tamoxifen is probably 5 years for protection against breast cancer.

OTHER DRUGS

A new class of drugs for treating breast cancer, called the aromatase inhibitors, has become available within the last few years and they are proving to be very beneficial treatments. Basically, they are used in women who are postmenopausal and they act by blocking the production of oestrogen that is still made in considerable quantities in these women. In blocking the production of oestrogen, they deprive any breast cancer cells of oestrogen, which acts as a stimulant. This is the only way that their action is similar to the effect of tamoxifen, but they can work after tamoxifen has failed to control the tumour. Aromatase inhibitors are so well tolerated that they are now being looked at as alternatives to tamoxifen in treatment of early disease.

Progestogens are also used to treat breast cancer in a large number of patients and are often used after initial therapy with tamoxifen, or one of the new aromatase inhibitors, has failed. The mechanism of action of progesterone is complex and poorly understood, but the drugs do have a very good track record over many years for controlling the disease.

The main reasons why tamoxifen or the aromatase inhibitors are chosen ahead of the progestogens are the side-effects. These are mild or minimal with the former but can be more troublesome, with weight gain

Side-effects of Drug Treatments

Unfortunately, many anti-cancer drugs have unpleasant side-effects, the commonest of which are listed below. However, a patient may not necessarily suffer from any or all of the side-effects.

HORMONE THERAPY	Toxicity.
OVARIAN ABLATION	Menopausal flushes and sweats, joint stiffness, lower libido and vaginal dryness.
TAMOXIFEN	The effects above plus weight gain, transient nausea, effects on the eyes, endometrial cancer risk, thromboembolic complications.
SPECIFIC AROMATASE INHIBITORS	As for ovarian ablation plus nausea.
PROGESTERONE	Increase in appetite, weight gain, vaginal bleeding, thromboembolism.
SPECIFIC ANTI-OESTROGENS	No menopausal flushing or sweating, etc.

being the major problem, with the high-dose progestogens. A glance at the box of side-effects of drug treatments (see above) gives some insight into the most common side-effects that are seen with hormone therapy, and which drugs are especially associated with those particular side-effects.

CHEMOTHERAPY

This treatment involves being given a combination of anti-cancer drugs, often three at a time. The prime target for such drugs is meant to be identifying and killing cells that are actively growing and dividing. Unfortunately, anti-cancer drugs are not able to recognise cancer cells specifically and they will kill other actively dividing cells such as cells of the blood or bone marrow (and hair). The bone marrow is an extremely important tissue in the body because it produces the blood cells and the cells of the immune system that fight infection. Drugs that destroy these cells result in complications such as anaemia, tendency to infection and problems with blood clotting resulting in a tendency to bleed after minor trauma.

The main problems with the blood, however, concern the white cells that are part of our defence against infection – there is such a big turnover in the number of white cells in the blood that they are particularly sensitive to the damage that is caused by toxic chemotherapy drugs.

The art and science behind successful cancer chemotherapy are to be found in the combination of drugs used, which is chosen in order to minimise the damage to the blood whilst maximising the damage to the cancer cells.

Sometimes chemotherapy is administered prior to surgery in order to shrink the tumour. This is so that the surgeon operating on the patient can leave more of the breast undamaged.

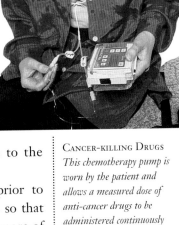

CANCER-KILLING DRUGS
This chemotherapy pump is worn by the patient and allows a measured dose of anti-cancer drugs to be administered continuously into a vein near the shoulder.

Cancer chemotherapy is usually given through an intravenous drip into your arm. It can be done on a outpatient basis, but some people prefer to stay in hospital overnight afterwards. Treatments vary but each session usually takes about half an hour and is repeated every three weeks. Some people prefer to stay the night in hospital after a treatment session, especially if they are very anxious. They may well be frightened of having chemotherapy because they have heard that there are very nasty side-effects, such as nausea, vomiting and hair loss. In fact, by no means everyone will experience all or even any of these problems. Some of the anti-cancer drugs now cause little or no hair thinning and anti-nausea medicines given with the chemotherapy work very well. Sedatives and/or anti-nausea drugs can be given through a drip if necessary.

One of the less well-known side-effects of chemo-therapy is to cause premature menopause in women who are still menstruating. This is particularly likely to occur in women in their late 30s and 40s, but even younger patients can temporarily have cessation of their periods as a result of the effects of chemo-therapy on the production of hormones by the ovaries. Typically, what happens in younger patients is recovery of periods after chemotherapy, but even then the natural menopause that follows may be brought forward by several years.

All this indicates is that, except in the youngest patients, chemotherapy is likely to impair fertility and some women who have delayed having children take active steps to attempt egg storage before chemo-therapy, so that they have the possibility of having a family after the breast cancer has been treated.

The most reliable way to achieve this is to be seen by a specialist in infertility medicine and to undergo storage of fertilised eggs (in vitro fertilisation or IVF). Experimentally, some units are now looking at the possibility of storing unfertilised eggs, but at the moment this is an unproved technique and it is unreliable.

STORING EGGS
Placing fertilised eggs in storage may be recommended for those women who need chemotherapy treatment, which can cause infertility.

Not all women under-going chemotherapy, however, will have their fertility impaired, so it is advisable that they avoid becoming pregnant by using a barrier method of contraception such as the condom because contraceptive pills can have an adverse effect on the breast cancer.

• **Intensive chemotherapy** In certain cases ordinary chemotherapy may not be adequate because the tumour is particularly aggressive, and very intensive treatment may be needed to wipe out all the tumour cells. The drug dose has to be so high that it also destroys the cells in the person's bone marrow and, to counter this, healthy cells can be removed from the bone marrow before the chemotherapy and then given back afterwards.

Although intensive chemotherapy does involve an element of risk, it may be the best option for someone who has very aggressive tumour, and clinical trials of this technique are being carried out in Europe at the moment.

HRT

Thus chemotherapy and hormone therapy can produce menopausal symptoms and may indeed artificially induce permanent menopause. Many patients ask whether it is possible just to take HRT to relieve the unpleasant symptoms of the menopause. The advice at most centres is not to take HRT, until alternatives have been tried, although the facts are that no one knows whether HRT adversely affects the breast cancer or not. The problem is that HRT is made up of low doses of oestrogen which, in theory, can stimulate some forms of breast cancer to grow again. Trials are being undertaken to see whether HRT can be used safely but the answers will not be available for some years. There are other ways of alleviating menopausal symptoms caused by anti-cancer treatments, sometimes involving drugs such as low dose progesterones and sometimes trying to alter lifestyle such as wearing clothes that tend to reduce sweating (loose and made of natural, rather than synthetic, fibres).

OTHER TREATMENTS
Medicines prepared by an Ayurvedic doctor, or other forms of complementary treatment, may be used in conjunction with conventional medicine, but be sure to consult your GP.

COMPLEMENTARY MEDICINE

Most doctors are concerned about the idea of people with breast cancer opting solely for alternative medicine when their disease is so eminently sensitive to conventional treatment. Nevertheless, many people find great comfort in having some input into the control of their condition by visiting herbalists or other practitioners of so-called natural medicines.

The commonsense approach is to discuss this openly and honestly with your GP. He or she is unlikely to raise any objections, provided that you do not opt for complementary medicine instead of conventional medical treatment.

WHEN A CURE IS NOT POSSIBLE

Despite the best efforts of the medical and surgical teams, some women with breast cancer will go on to develop advanced disease that cannot be cured. Even when this does happen, however, there is still an enormous amount that can be done to help both the woman herself and her family.

It is nearly always possible to control symptoms such as pain and nausea and the palliative care team will have all the necessary expertise. In this context, the palliative care team can advise either the GP or the hospital oncology department about the optimum use of drugs such as pain killers, drugs that combat nausea and diarrhoea, and to maximise the patient's appetite, which can often be poor as a result of the illness or the treatment. It should be remembered that the main aim of the intervention on behalf of the palliative team is to give the patient the best possible quality of life with the minimum symptoms of the disease and the minimum side-effects of treatment.

For more information about organisations that can provide information and support in this situation, see pp.90–92.

KEY POINTS

- Synthetic hormones are very effective drugs for treating hormone-sensitive breast cancer.
- Chemotherapy doses and schedules are optimised to give the best anti-cancer effect while causing the minimum damage to the normal tissues.
- Palliative treatment of breast cancer is often done in conjunction with an expert care team whose aim is to improve the patient's quality of life.

Personal reactions

Any breast problem, even one that is minor in health terms, is likely to affect a woman psychologically and emotionally as well as physically. Very many women are sensitive about the shape and size of their breasts, and of course breasts are an important aspect of any woman's sexuality.

Both men and women perceive breasts in a sexual way and a woman may be concerned about her partner's likely reaction to any breast problem, as well as her own.

From her own perspective, anything being wrong with her breasts may have a damaging effect on her self-image and so take on an importance way beyond its significance in pure health terms. Of course, no two women will react in exactly the same way and your reaction to any breast problem is unique, but knowing that these kind of worries are normal may help to keep them in proportion.

THE EMOTIONAL RESPONSE
The psychological impact of breast cancer can be devastating. The loss of a breast can be a major blow to a woman's self-esteem.

Doctors and nurses who treat women with all kinds of breast problems are well aware of the psychological aspects of breast disease. Usually, they will ask about your emotional reactions and whether you have any worries you would like to talk over and it really is worth taking the opportunity to raise anything that is on your mind. Some people find this difficult, perhaps feeling that nothing can be done to help or that they would be wasting the professionals' time. This is very much not the case, and keeping your concerns to yourself is likely to do more harm than good in the long run.

You should be offered support and advice by the doctors and nurses involved in your care, but there are also numerous support groups that can offer something more for those who want it. In particular, there is a lot of help available for women who have breast cancer and their families, including the opportunity to meet and talk to others in a similar situation. This is usually someone who has breast cancer treated successfully and has had some training in helping other people cope. More details can be found in the next section.

GETTING SUPPORT
Self-help groups can prove to be a valuable source of emotional support, as can your specialised care team.

When it is a member of your family or close friend who has a serious condition such as breast cancer, it can be hard to express your worries or seek emotional support for yourself. Many relatives believe that they must not compete with the patient's need for help even though they may have as many, or more, concerns. There are now groups to help relatives cope with breast cancer.

KEY POINTS

- Breast conditions can often affect women psychologically and emotionally.
- Do not keep your concerns to yourself, but share them with your carers.
- Support should be available from your doctors and nurses, and is also available from self-help groups.

Useful addresses

Support groups

If you would like to talk to someone else who has been through similar experiences, trained volunteers can be contacted through Breast Cancer Care (see below) or local self-help groups. The following national associations provide emotional support and practical help to women with breast cancer or her friends and relatives.

Breast Cancer Care (BCC)

Formerly known at the Breast Care and Mastectomy Association for Great Britain
The organisation offers free help and information for women with breast cancer and other breast diseases. They also produce a range of information leaflets on care and prostheses.
BCC helplines:
London (0500) 245 345
Glasgow (0141) 221 2233

Or write to:
Kiln House
210 New King's Road
London SW6 4NZ
or
Suite 2/8,
46 Gordon Street
Glasgow G1 3PU

British Association of Cancer United Patients (BACUP)

This gives advice and information about all aspects of cancer as well as emotional support for individuals affected by breast cancer and their families and friends. Their cancer information service is staffed by a team of specially trained nurses and supported by a panel of medical specialists. A cancer counselling service is available to anyone who wishes to travel to their offices in London or Glasgow. BACUP help and information lines.
Cancer information service:
London (0171) 696 9003
Outside London: Freeline: (0800) 181199
Counselling service:
London (0171) 696 9000
Glasgow (0141) 553 1553

Or write to:
3 Bath Place
Rivington Street
London EC2A 3DR

Cancer Care Society

The Cancer Care Society (CARE) offers counselling and emotional support and practical information, rather than medical support, for patients and their families and friends.
Tel: (0117) 9427419

CancerLink

This is for any individual with cancer, not just women with breast cancer. Their information service offers support and they can help anyone given options for treatment by providing information that allows you to make an informed decision.
CancerLink help and information lines:
London (0171) 833 2451
Freephone: (0800) 132905

Asian language information and support line (Hindi, Bengali, Gujerati, Punjabi, Urdu and Cantonese): (0171) 713 7867.

Or write to:
CancerLink
11–21 Northdown Street
London N1 9BW
or
CancerLink
9 Castle Terrace
Edinburgh EH1 2DP

Macmillan Cancer Relief

This organisation has compiled a list of specialist breast units and specialist breast surgeons in the UK. Write for a copy to:
15–19 Britten Street
London SW3 3TZ

Macmillan Cancer Relief nurses provide a link for hospices, GPs and the Cancer Centre or Cancer Unit. They can be contacted through Macmillan Cancer Relief.

Women's Nationwide Cancer Control Campaign (WNCCC)

The main aims of this campaign are early detection and prevention and a nationwide clinic list for anyone wanting to find her nearest one. Their helpline provides information and emotional support on breast screening. They do not deal with queries about established cancer or its treatment.
WNCCC helpline: (0171) 729 2229

Or write to:
Suna House
128–130 Curtain Road
London EC2A 3AR

Social Security benefits

Details of social security benefits available to women are available by contacting:
National Association of Citizens'
Advice Bureaux
115–123 Pentonville Road
London N1 9LZ

or look in the local telephone directory for the address of the nearest local Citizens' Advice Bureaux. There are 1,500 Bureaux nationwide and all these can provide free, impartial, confidential advice and help. Most specialist units have access to support funds and can help people who want to apply.

Notes

Index

93

Acknowledgements

PUBLISHER'S ACKNOWLEDGEMENTS
Dorling Kindersley would like to thank the following for their help
and participation in this project:

Production Assistant Elizabeth Cherry; **Consultancy** Dr. Sue Davidson;
Indexing Indexing Specialists, Hove; **Administration** Christopher Gordon.

Illustrations Neal Johnson (p.11, p.17, p.24),
© Philip Wilson (p.9, p.22, p.70, p.73), Fiona Roberts (p.60).

Picture research Angela Anderson; **Picture Librarian** Charlotte Oster.

PICTURE CREDITS
The publisher would like to thank the following for their kind
permission to reproduce their photographs. Every effort has been made
to trace the copyright holders. Dorling Kindersley apologises for any
unintentional omissions and would be pleased, in any such cases,
to add an acknowledgement in future editions.

APM Studio p.32, p.33
Collections p.43 (Anthea Sieveking);
National Medical Slide Bank p.28 top, p.44, p.49, p.50;
Science Photo Library p.3 & 15 & jacket (King's College School of Medicine),
p.14 (Chris Priest), p.20 (Hattie Young), p.26 (King's College School of Medicine),
p.30 (Dr. P. Marazzi), p.45 (Dr. P. Marazzi), p.53 (Breast Screening Unit,
King's College Hospital), p.55 (Chris Bjornberg), p.63 & jacket (Nancy Kedersha),
p.65 (BSIP, Laurent H. Americain), p.68 (BSIP Boucharlat), p.69 (King's College School
of Medicine), p.81 (James King-Holmes), p.83 (Hank Morgan), p.87 (BSIP Chassenet);
Telegraph Colour Library p.19 & jacket (R. Chapple);
Tony Stone Images p.16 (Ben Edwards).